# Popular Culture:
# 1980–1999

Jilly Hunt

**www.raintreepublishers.co.uk**
Visit our website to find out
more information about
Raintree books.

**To order:**
☎ Phone 0845 6044371
🖹 Fax +44 (0) 1865 312263
✉ Email myorders@raintreepublishers.co.uk

Customers from outside the UK please telephone +44 1865 312262

Raintree is an imprint of Capstone Global Library
Limited, a company incorporated in England and Wales
having its registered office at 7 Pilgrim Street, London,
EC4V 6LB – Registered company number: 6695582

Edited by Adam Miller, Andrew Farrow, and
  Adrian Vigliano
Designed by Richard Parker
Original illustrations © Capstone Global Ltd 2013
Illustrations by Richard Parker
Picture research by Mica Brancic
Originated by Capstone Global Library Ltd
Printed and bound in China by Leo Paper Products Ltd

ISBN 978 1 406 24024 5 (hardback)
16 15 14 13 12
10 9 8 7 6 5 4 3 2 1

**British Library Cataloguing in Publication Data**
A full catalogue record for this book is available from
the British Library.

**Acknowledgments**
We would like to thank the following for permission to
reproduce photographs: Corbis pp. 21 (epa/© Ferdinand
Ostrop), 25 (Sygma/© Julio Donoso), 24 (Loop Images/
LOOP IMAGES/© Picture Hooked), 32 (© Steve
Schapiro); Getty Images pp. 5 (Doug Pensinger), 7
(Apic), 6 (Gamma-Rapho/Pool APESTEGUY/HIRES),
8 (Redferns/Richard E. Aaron), 11 (Redferns/Mike
Cameron), 15 (WireImage/Kevin Mazur), 16 (Redferns/
Des Willie), 19 (Janette Beckman), 35 (The Washington
Post/Lois Raimondo), 36 (Liaison/Jonathan Elderfield),
38 (Michael Grecco), 39 (Science & Society Picture
Library), 43 (Redferns/David Redfern), 44 (Dave M.
Bennett), 46 (Michael Putland), 49 (Hulton Archive/
Michael Putland), 48 (Michael Ochs Archives), 50 (AFP
Photo/Maria R. Bastone), 52 (Science & Society Picture
Library); The Kobal Collection pp. 27 (20th Century
Fox/Paramount), 28 (Lucasfilm); Press Association p.
47 (Empics Entertainment/Anwar Hussein); Reuters
p. 23 (© Kieran Doherty); Rex Features pp. 4 (David
Thorpe), 13 (PYMCA/Peter J Walsh), 29 (HERBERT),
31 (SNAP), 33 (Everett Collection), 41 (Tim Rooke).
Background images and design features reproduced
with permission of Shutterstock.

Cover photograph of breakdancers reproduced with the
permission of Getty Images (Michael Ochs Archives).

Every effort has been made to contact copyright holders
of any material reproduced in this book. Any omissions
will be rectified in subsequent printings if notice is
given to the publisher.

**Disclaimer**
All the Internet addresses (URLs) given in this book
were valid at the time of going to press. However, due to
the dynamic nature of the Internet, some addresses may
have changed, or sites may have changed or ceased to
exist since publication. While the author and publisher
regret any inconvenience this may cause readers, no
responsibility for any such changes can be accepted by
either the author or the publisher.

# Contents

Some words are printed in bold, **like this**. You can find out what they mean by looking in the glossary.

# What is popular culture?

What do you enjoy doing in your free time? Do you enjoy listening to music or playing computer games? Do you enjoy watching films? Or perhaps you like flipping through the pages of a magazine to find out about the latest fashions? Chances are that a lot of other people like the same films, television, music, games, books, or magazines as you. This makes these pastimes part of a popular culture.

The word *culture* can be used in many ways, but in this book we mean culture to be the arts, such as film, music, books, and design. Culture can also include elements that are part of everyday life, such as travel and the clothes people wear.

## Where does popular culture start?

Popular culture might be different in different countries or there might be trends that appeal to lots of people around the world. Sometimes a trend is linked to an invention, such as the Internet, and it appeals to everyone and becomes a part of popular culture. The World Wide Web changed people's lives halfway through the 1990s as it enabled them to shop online. For the first time ever people could order books or music from new websites such as Amazon, or sell their unwanted goods on auction websites such as eBay.

The Rubik's cube filled many a frustrated hour in the 1980s as people tried to figure out how to get all of the same colour squares on to the same side of the cube.

# Popular youth culture in the 1980s and 1990s

In the 1980s and 1990s, young people would spend their time listening to rap on their **boom boxes** or perhaps pop on their Sony Walkmans. They might go to the local video arcade to play video games such as *Donkey Kong* or *Pac-Man* or, later in the decade, go to their friends' houses to play *Dungeons and Dragons* or *The Legend of Zelda* on their home computer.

BMX biking, skateboarding, and inline skating were fun and fashionable. Roller discos were at their peak in the 1980s but had virtually disappeared by the end of the 1990s. Special effects and computer-generated images (CGI) in films impressed cinema-goers, and 3-D films tried to make *Jaws 3* even scarier.

Skateboarding was all the rage in the 1990s.

# What was the world like in the 1980s and 1990s?

The 1980s was a time of strikes and job losses, with factories and mines shutting down and an economic recession leading to high unemployment. But business was booming in finance, with **yuppies** seeming to get rich quick. That was until the stock markets collapsed on Black Monday, 19 October 1987, in the United States,[1] and Black Wednesday, 16 September 1992, in the United Kingdom.[2]

## Politics

Margaret Thatcher became the first female British prime minister in 1979 and governed until 1990. She earned the nickname Iron Lady from the Soviet press because of her strong anticommunist beliefs.[3] In the United States, former film star Ronald Reagan became president in 1980 and governed until 1988, when Vice President George H. W. Bush won the election. Together with Thatcher, Reagan ensured the **Cold War** continued. The Cold War had started between the Soviet Union and the United States following the end of World War II. The war was fought mainly on political and economic fronts, not on a battlefield. The Cold War began to break down in the late 1980s, when Mikhail Gorbachev became leader of the Soviet Union. Gorbachev introduced reforms into the Soviet Union that eventually led to the collapse of the union in 1991.

In 1993, Bill Clinton became president of the United States and oversaw the country's longest peacetime economic expansion.[4] In 1997, Tony Blair became the youngest prime minister of Britain since 1812.[5]

In the early 1980s, Ronald Reagan and Margaret Thatcher maintained a strong anticommunist stance against the Soviet Union.

## Fall of the Berlin Wall

The building of the Berlin Wall started in August 1961.[6] It separated communist East Germany from the democratic West Germany. The Berlin Wall came to represent the Cold War's division of Eastern from Western Europe. In October 1989, East Germany's communist leadership was forced out of power, and by November 1989, the East German borders were open and people could travel freely across them. This opened up the channels for a spread of culture. Western world culture could now influence the previously isolated Eastern European countries.

# First Gulf War, 1990–1991

The First Gulf War started after Iraq invaded its neighbour, Kuwait. Saddam Hussein was the president of Iraq at the time. The United States, under President George H. W. Bush, and its allies used military force to defeat Hussein.[7]

# Disasters

During this period there was a series of natural and human-made disasters, which made people think more about the environment. For example, the explosion at the Chernobyl nuclear reactor in the Soviet Union in 1986,[8] spread radioactive pollution across the Soviet Union and Western Europe.

In 1986 the US space shuttle programme was temporarily grounded following the explosion of the space shuttle *Challenger*, which killed all crew members aboard, including Christa McAuliffe, a school teacher.

# Music

In the 1980s and 1990s, there was a wide range of Western music styles available to play, from pop to heavy metal to grunge to Britpop. Music played a big role in popular culture and influenced how people dressed, what magazines they bought, what clubs they went to, and what radio or TV stations they tuned in to.

## Pop, new wave, and metal

The popular charts were dominated by big name pop stars, such as Madonna, Prince, Michael Jackson, Whitney Houston, George Michael, and Janet Jackson. These artists had a strong visual appeal and were helped by the rise of the music video. When a new company called MTV began broadcasting music videos in the United States in 1981,[1] it was no longer enough just to be a talented musician. Innovative videos helped sell the music, and a strong image was essential.

Prince's popularity helped to break down the racial barriers imposed by MTV.

## Breaking down boundaries

MTV and many radio stations in the United States had racially defined boundaries for what music they played. At first, MTV's policy was to play very few videos from black musicians. This policy was questioned by people in the music industry, such as rock legend David Bowie. Eventually the president of CBS Records threatened to prevent MTV from playing any of his label's music unless the policy was dropped. Such pressures, combined with the spectacular success of Michael Jackson's *Thriller* (1982) and Prince's *Little Red Corvette* (1982) and *Purple Rain* (1984),[2] helped to break down these boundaries.

New wave music included a variety of styles, such as The Human League, Heaven 17, and A Flock of Seagulls. In the United States, new wave included the B-52s, the Go-Go's, the Cars, Devo, and Talking Heads. Also grouped with new wave were **ska** revivalist groups Madness and the Specials, and the new romantics such as Duran Duran, Culture Club, and Adam and the Ants. The new romantics were distinguished by their clothing and for male band members who wore make-up. By the mid-1980s, the division between new wave and mainstream pop became smaller with the success of many new wave groups, such as U2, the Police, and the Pretenders.

By the end of the 1980s, heavy metal had become the dominant **genre** in pop.[3] Bands such as Iron Maiden, Def Leppard, Motley Crüe, Poison, Van Halen, and Bon Jovi received significant radio exposure. When MTV first aired *Headbangers Ball* in 1987, it became hugely popular.[4] The success of these bands was down to a mix of catchy songs, high production values (quality of the video or performance), some glamour, and often a balance of pop romance and rock rebellion. Many of these bands were nicknamed hair metal because of their make-up, big hair, and colourful, tight spandex clothing.

## Did you know?

The Guns N' Roses album *Appetite for Destruction* is a mix of heavy metal with punk rock elements. It made a big impact when it was released in 1987 and has become one of the best-selling albums of all time in the United States.

## Rise of the CD

How do you buy your music? Do you walk into a shop and buy a CD or album? Or do you download a song from the Internet? In the 1980s, the compact disc (CD) was the latest way of buying music. Before this, vinyl records and audio cassettes, or tapes, were the popular ways of buying and playing music. Within 10 years of the CD being introduced, the sales of CDs had overtaken the sales of vinyl records.[5]

The popularity of the CD had an interesting effect on the sales of popular music. It created a market for older audiences who bought CDs to replace their old vinyl records. This meant that many pop stars from the 1960s had their careers extended. You would imagine that the success of the CD would mean the end of vinyl records. However, a cult market has grown up around them for those who admire the old vinyl records, and their packaging design. The audio cassette didn't last though!

## Music on the move

The Sony Walkman cassette player was introduced in 1979.[6] It might seem big compared to today's MP3 players, but when the Walkman was released it was a huge success and sold hundreds of millions of units.[7]

## Experimentation with sounds

In the mid-1980s, a technique called **sampling** became popular, creating a shift in music styles. Sampling is a process where a sound is taken from one recording and used on a new recording. Musicians could now combine new and old music together. By the 1990s, sampling was a common technique in music such as rap and rock.

Other new technology that became widely available in the 1980s included drum machines, synthesizers, personal computers, and sequencers, which create repeatable sequences of sound.[8] This new technology allowed musicians to create a wide variety of sounds digitally. It became common to not see any traditional instruments when watching a band play. Instead, viewers would watch a band, such as the Pet Shop Boys, where someone was standing behind a keyboard and someone else was singing.

## Live Aid

In the mid-1980s, the music industry came together to raise money for the people suffering from Ethiopia's years of drought and famine. UK musicians Bob Geldof and Midge Ure wrote a song that was recorded by some of the biggest names in British music. In 1984, "Do They Know It's Christmas?" sold over three million copies and encouraged musicians around the world to support the cause. Harry Belafonte organized USA for Africa's single "We Are the World" in January 1985. And in July 1985, there was a benefit concert held simultaneously in London and Philadelphia called Live Aid. It attracted about 1.5 billion television viewers and raised millions of pounds.[9]

## Dance music

One of the styles of music that used technology heavily was dance music. Dance music can be traced to the mid-1970s and the **hip-hop** crews of New York (see pages 18–19). Hip-hop DJs used tracks from vinyl records along with **scratching** and mixing techniques, and then later incorporated synthesizers and drum machines. The rap and hip-hop style was introduced to a mainstream audience by acts such as the Sugarhill Gang and Grandmaster Flash and the Furious Five.

## House

House music is high-tempo, electronic dance music that started in Chicago, Illinois, in the early 1980s.[10] The name "house" came from the Warehouse Nightclub in Chicago and its resident DJ, Frankie Knuckles.[11] The original house sound is a mix of 1970s disco, Eurodisco, psychedelia, and old soul hits.[12] The style had spread to Europe by 1986, with "Jack Your Body", by Chicago-based Steve "Silk" Hurley, becoming the first house record to become a hit in the UK pop charts.[13] This was followed by "Pump Up the Volume" by the UK group M/A/R/R/S in 1987.[14]

A **subculture** of house music developed called acid house. In Britain, as well as the rest of Europe, Australia, and South Africa, this created an explosion in the youth culture as it became part of the rave scene. In Britain, raves involved illegal parties and were linked to the drug ecstasy.

### Madchester and Factory Records

The city of Manchester and its surrounding areas were home to some unique bands of the era, such as Happy Mondays, The Stone Roses, The Charlatans, A Guy Called Gerald, James, and the Inspiral Carpets. The scene became known as Madchester. The Hacienda nightclub in Manchester was the centre of the scene. It was set up in 1982 by Tony Wilson and Factory Records and the band New Order.[15] The Hacienda remained open until 1997.

Factory Records and its founder, Tony Wilson, had a huge impact on the British music scene. It signed influential bands such as Joy Division in the late 1970s, who went on to become New Order, and Happy Mondays. New Order's "Blue Monday" became the biggest-selling 12-inch record in the United Kingdom. Despite this success, Factory Records lost money on the sale of every copy because of the expensive sleeve design. It went bankrupt in 1992.[16]

Following a crackdown by police on after-hours house parties, secret raves were organized, often taking place in warehouses and other hidden venues. Raves appealed to people from different backgrounds, including many young middle-class professionals.

A new style of music developed because of this rave scene. Dancers would need a place to chill out and clubs would have an area for this in which ambient house music was playing. Ambient house was calming and relaxing. Artists such as the Orb, Aphex Twin, and 808 State were involved in producing these chillout tunes.

The main dance floor of Manchester's Hacienda was the place to be for much of the 1980s and 1990s.

## Alternative music

While the major record labels in the 1980s and 1990s focused on the promotion of consistent megastars such as Michael Jackson and Madonna, their dominance in the market declined as smaller independent labels grew in popularity.[17] During this era, the music industry saw the rise of alternative music. Bands that had no chance of being signed to a major record label forged an independent network of like-minded clubs, record labels, writers, and fans. This indie (short for "independent") scene increased in popularity as the music reflected the feelings of its generation. This generation became known as Generation X.[18] There was a rise in unemployment and decline in decent wages. The feelings of this generation are reflected in alternative music, with its themes of loss of faith and distrustful attitudes towards modern life.

## The rise of the indie scene

The indie network was established by the American hardcore punk scene. Bands such as Black Flag, Minor Threat, and the Dead Kennedys were part of an underground punk movement across the United States in the early 1980s.[19] Punkers, with their **DIY ethics**, wanted to do everything themselves, from recording the music to producing albums and merchandise, to distributing the work, and even deciding where they performed, often in residential homes. This established the indie scene with independent venues and record labels, such as SST and Dischord. It became increasingly possible for bands without a major record contract to play for national audiences.

## Grunge

Grunge was influenced by punk rock and heavy metal, and mixed guitar with anguished vocals and angst-ridden lyrics. The style developed in Seattle, Washington, and came to the attention of the mainstream with the success of Nirvana's *Nevermind* album in 1991. The album sold over 10 million copies.[20] Other Seattle grunge bands became more prominent on the back of Nirvana's success, such as Mudhoney, Soundgarden, and Pearl Jam. The label "grunge" was also given to Stone Temple Pilots and Dinosaur Jr., bands from cities other than Seattle. Grunge also had links with "riot grrrl" music from bands with all-female lineups, such as Bikini Kill and Bratmobile. Grunge took the place of popular heavy metal or hair metal.

## Kurt Cobain (1967-1994)

Kurt Cobain was born near Seattle, Washington, in 1967 and formed Nirvana with Chad Channing and Krist Novoselic in 1986 (Dave Grohl replaced Channing in 1990). Kurt Cobain was thought of as the voice of his generation, but he was very uncomfortable with fame and success, and also suffered from problems such as drug addiction and depression. However, he was a celebrity, and the media constantly featured stories about him and his wife, Courtney Love from the band Hole, and their heroin use. In 1994, Kurt committed suicide.[21]

## Britpop

While grunge was growing in the United States, many young Britons reacted against the harsh sounds and "nevermind" attitude of the performers. Britpop developed in the early 1990s as a British reaction to the "invasion" of US grunge bands.[22] Bands such as Blur and Suede reacted to the grunge dominance with a celebration of their origins, while Blur also began a mission "to get rid of grunge".[23] They were interested in making music that was unmistakably British.

The term *Britpop* was first used in the British music press in 1992,[24] and described guitar-based bands that originated from the British indie music scene. It included groups such as Suede, Oasis, Pulp, and Blur, who played indie-inspired pop. It revolved largely around the Camden Town area of London.

Pulp performing on television in 1994. Britpop bands became increasingly popular and influential in the US as well as the UK.

Nostalgia influenced Britpop, as bands returned to traditional instruments and valued the craft of songwriting. Musicians looked to 1960s British bands, including the Beatles, the Kinks, and T. Rex for inspiration. Britpop bands were followed by new British bands such as experimental rockers Radiohead, who released their first album in 1993, and Coldplay. Both bands have gone on to have huge success around the world.

While fans of guitar-based rock were listening to Britpop bands, many other music lovers were becoming "boy band" fans. The US group New Kids on the Block released their first album in 1986 and became a huge sensation until they broke up in 1994. New Kids on the Block were followed by US groups such as Backstreet Boys and *NSYNC, while in the UK, groups such as Take That ruled the charts. In 1996, the Spice Girls challenged boy band superiority with their internationally successful debut album.

## Battle of the bands

By 1995, the British press had built up an intense rivalry between Manchester's Oasis and London's Blur.[25] Both bands were trying to become successful in the United States as well as in the United Kingdom. The bands' record labels decided to build on this rivalry by releasing their new singles on the same day. The newspaper coverage turned it into a class war between the southern, middle-class educated Blur and the northern, working-class Oasis. Blur's "Country House" single outsold Oasis's "Roll With It".[26] However, the pressure from this artificial battle nearly drove Graham Coxon from Blur to suicide,[27] and Oasis eventually went on to become much more popular than Blur in the United States.

### Noel (1967-) and Liam Gallagher (1972-)

Brothers Noel and Liam Gallagher from Manchester formed the group Oasis in 1992. They signed with the indie label Creation and released their first single "Supersonic" in 1994. Noel Gallagher had previously been a **roadie** for Inspiral Carpets, and their early music shows the influence of Madchester bands and the Beatles. Noel was the main songwriter of the group, while Liam was the front man who built up a swaggering, hard-man-of-pop image. Their first album, *Definitely Maybe* (1994), followed by (*What's the Story) Morning Glory?* (1995) and *Be Here Now* (1997), made Oasis one of the most commercially successful British bands of the 1990s. They were also one of the few Britpop bands to find success on the international stage.[28]

# Hip-hop, New York style

A new and distinct New York style developed in the late 1960s and early 1970s but really made an impact in the 1980s. This New York style was part of the hip-hop culture that included DJing, rapping, break dancing, and graffiti. Early hip-hop was an underground movement, but it came to the attention of a more mainstream audience with the release of films in the 1980s such as *Beat Street, Wild Style*, and the documentary *Style Wars*.

New York style started in the poor, predominantly African American South Bronx area of New York. This subculture was heavily influenced by features of African American culture, including the style of characters found in New York graffiti and the rapping elements of hip-hop.

## Graffiti

New York City is considered "the capital and cultural centre of graffiti", according to artists Henry Chalfant and James Prigoff. This is where young writers created a new art form that spread around the world. Graffiti first appeared on the streets of New York when kids started **tagging** (writing their street name or tag) on neighbourhood walls and street signs. But New York style is really associated with the subway and its trains. In the 1970s and 1980s, graffiti writers such as Lee Quinones and Dondi White used subway trains to get their work and their names known around the city. Certain train lines were better than others because of the wider route they took, enabling the writers to communicate with others in different **boroughs**. These trains would be used by the more talented and, therefore, most respected writers.

## DJing, rapping, and break dancing

As with graffiti, the musical element of hip-hop developed in inner city New York. DJ Kool Herc, an 18-year-old Jamaican **immigrant**,[1] brought over huge sound systems from Jamaica and introduced them to New York's inner city parties. DJ Kool Herc, along with others such as Grand Wizard Theodore, Afrika Bambaataa, and Grandmaster Flash, pioneered the hip-hop sound. These DJs were creating new techniques for using **turntables** and experimenting with sound. Grand Wizard Theodore originated needle dropping, or isolating and extending the **break beat**, and scratching. These sounds encouraged the **improvised**, acrobatic dance style called break dancing. Contests evolved where individual dancers would try to outdo each other with the best moves they had.

Rapping is when the DJ or rapper speaks over the record. The rapping part of hip-hop is heavily influenced by such elements of African American culture as talking blues songs and the late 1960s and early 1970s black power poetry of artists such as Gil Scott-Heron and Amiri Baraka.[2] Gil Scott-Heron became known as the Godfather of Rap (although he didn't like the term), because of his influential spoken-word performances set to music.[3]

The hip-hop artists Rock Steady Crew helped bring the music and art of the New York City style to a more mainstream audience. They are seen here break dancing.

## Language

The New York graffiti culture developed its own language. Here are some examples:

| | |
|---|---|
| **bite** | to copy someone else's style |
| **bomb** | to do lots of graffiti |
| **crew** | group of writers |
| **wildstyle** | interlocking letters |

# Art

In the art world, the 1980s saw the continuation of conceptual art from the 1970s. This is artwork based on an idea or a concept and isn't always what the general public regards as traditional art. Many might question whether it is art at all. In the 1980s, there was a new generation of conceptual artists, which included Sherrie Levine, Barbara Kruger, and Jenny Holzer. There was also a return to more traditional figure painting and sculpture, with artists such as Anselm Kiefer, Georg Baselitz, and Elizabeth Murray.

## The appeal of the poster

One poster, titled "Man and Baby", seemed to capture the hearts of teenage girls and women in the 1980s. The poster, made by the former company Athena, is of a male model holding a newborn baby, and it sold five million copies, making the company millions of dollars.[1] This poster, along with others such as "Che Guevara", "Tennis Girl", and "The Kiss" by Robert Doisneau, adorned the walls of many 1980s and 1990s bedrooms. But there was a debate about whether they were truly art.

## Popular culture and art

Popular culture influenced the work of many artists in the 1980s and 1990s. Their subject matter was often taken from popular culture. The American artist Jeff Koons took familiar, everyday items and gave them art status. For example, he encased vacuum cleaners in Lucite, turning them into monuments. The irony was that a product that is made for cleaning is kept dust-free, never to be used. Koons liked to produce public sculptures so that many people could see his work. He created replicas of familiar items and played with the scale to produce oversized versions, such as his "Puppy" (1992), which was as tall as a building and covered in living flowers.[2] Koons used figures from the celebrity world to create sculptures, such as the one of Michael Jackson and his pet chimpanzee, Bubbles, from 1988.[3] Koons wanted his work to reach a wide audience, and choosing a very famous pop star made his work more interesting to the everyday person.

Jeff Koon's porcelain figure of Michael Jackson with his pet chimpanzee, Bubbles, was auctioned off for $5.6 million.

American photographer Cindy Sherman made herself part of popular culture by taking pictures of herself in the pop culture settings of TV soaps, old films, and magazines. Richard Prince used imagery from magazine advertisements in his artwork. Between 1980 and 1992, Prince took photos of a cowboy who was used in a high-profile advertising campaign for cigarettes and used them to question the ideals behind the American dream. The cowboy was still an idealized symbol of American life and many thought the photos showed how this and the American Dream itself were only a myth.[4]

## Britart

In London, from the 1980s to the late 1990s, there was a talented group of young artists working mainly in the conceptual style of art, which became known as Britart.[5] The group, ultimately known as Young British Artists (**YBAs**), included Damien Hirst, Rachel Whiteread, Chris Ofili, and Tracey Emin. Their work might have gone unnoticed were it not for people in the art world and interested members of the general public. Fortunately, this group of artists was in the right place at the right time.

In addition to being talented, the group was excellent at self-promotion and knew how to manipulate the media to get attention. The first exhibition of these artists, *Freeze*, was organized by Damien Hirst and held in a warehouse in London in 1988. The fact that these young artists organized their own exhibition showed their independence. They also managed to attract the attention of Charles Saatchi, a famous art collector and co-founder of the international advertising agency Saatchi & Saatchi. He became a sponsor of the YBAs and helped bring the group to the attention of the media. In the early 1990s, there was a series of exhibitions called "Young British Artists" held at the Saatchi Gallery in London.

## The Turner Prize

In 1984, a new British art award called the **Turner Prize** was introduced at the Tate Gallery in London. The prize is considered to be the best in the British art world and aims to promote contemporary art. Several of the YBAs have been nominated for the Turner Prize. The prize caused controversy and often appeared in the media, capturing the interest of the British public. Debate arose about whether the work of the artists shortlisted for the prize was actually art.

## Headline-grabbing art

The art of the YBAs often grabbed the headlines because of its subject matter. Hirst's piece *Mother and Child Divided* (1995) was four glass and steel tanks each with the severed halves of a cow and calf. Was this art or was Hirst just trying to shock? In April 1998, Hirst's medicine cabinet, *God*, achieved a world record price by selling for £188,500.[6] The British public was fascinated.

**Did you know?**

Damien Hirst also directed the music video for Blur's "Country House" single.[7]

# Damien Hirst (1965-)

Damien Hirst was born in Bristol in 1965 and grew up in Leeds before he moved to London in the early 1980s. He attended Goldsmiths College in London, where he met other Young British Artists. His *Freeze* exhibition gained the attention of Charles Saatchi, who became one of Hirst's biggest collectors. Hirst was awarded the Turner Prize in 1995.[8] He has also been involved in pop music projects and interior designs for the restaurants Pharmacy and Quo Vadis in London. His recent works have reached record prices at auction.

## Street art

As in music, the influence of the New York City hip-hop scene with its street art style, or graffiti, soon spread around the world (see pages 18–19), although the graffiti mainly appeared as wall art, rather than on trains. The New York style spread through newspaper articles and exhibitions. New York's *Village Voice* featured an article on New York graffiti made by Lee Quinones and Fab 5 Freddy. An Italian art dealer, Claudio Bruni, saw this article and invited Lee and Fred to exhibit their paintings in his gallery in Rome.[9]

In the early 1980s, Dutch art dealer Yaki Kornblit held a breakthrough exhibition in Rotterdam featuring works by New York graffiti artists Dondi, Crash, Rammellzee, and other artists such as Futura 2000, Zephyr, Quik, Pink, Blade, Seen, and Bill Blast.[10] There were already many street taggers and writers in Holland, particularly in Amsterdam. Following this exhibition, street art in Amsterdam showed a strong New York connection.

British street artist Banksy started as a graffiti artist in the early 1990s, and eventually incoporated stencilling into his work. This photo shows a work of his made on the wall of an unused London Underground tunnel in 2008.

# Global influence

The New York style's influence spread to other cities around the world, such as London, Bristol, Sydney, Auckland, Paris, Copenhagen, Berlin, and Vienna. In each country, and each city, individual writers added and adapted the graffiti style to form their own styles. In the United Kingdom, graffiti found an underground home in cities such as London and Bristol. Artists such as 3D and Banksy originated from Bristol, Goldie from Wolverhampton, and Fade 2, Mode 2, and the Chrome Anglez from London.[11]

Jean-Michel Basquiat in front of his own work in January 1988. He died from an overdose in August 1988.

## Jean-Michel Basquiat (1960-1988) and Keith Haring (1958-1990)

Some graffiti artists caught the attention of the media. Jean-Michel Basquiat and Keith Haring were two such artists. Basquiat was born in Brooklyn, New York, in 1960,[12] but left home at 17. He lived on the streets in New York in abandoned buildings or with friends. He and two other graffiti artists, Al Diaz and Shannon Dawson, began to graffiti the streets of New York under the name SAMO©. Keith Haring was born in 1958 in Reading, Pennsylvania. He moved to New York in 1978[13] and became involved in the same street art scene as Basquiat. He had a different style to other graffiti artists. He would do chalk drawings on blank, black advertising panels in the New York subways. His lively style of figures and patterns quickly became popular.

# Film and TV

In the 1980s and 1990s, watching films at home became increasingly popular. The first video recorders were sold in 1979,[1] and with a trip to the local video rental shop, people could rent the latest films. Dolby surround sound was introduced in 1982,[2] which made the sound quality at home more like the sound at a cinema. In 1995,[3] DVDs became available and provided a sharper picture and better quality than videos, and they often contained interactive extras. The home movie experience was enjoyable and much cheaper than going out to the cinema.

## Blockbusters

Producing a film was becoming increasingly expensive, and cinema ticket prices were falling, so film companies didn't make as much money. Major film companies designed films to appeal to the majority of people. They wanted to make the biggest selling film they could, and that meant appealing to as many people as possible. Films that were designed for entertainment and thrills were known as blockbusters. Big blockbusters of the era included *E.T.: The Extra-Terrestrial*, *Titanic*, *Austin Powers*, *Mission: Impossible*, *Pretty Woman*, *Beverly Hills Cop*, and *Jurassic Park*. The British film *Four Weddings and a Funeral* was a huge success as well. Its quirky plot appealed to audiences and it became a worldwide hit with earnings of more than $258 million.[4]

## Sequels

Film companies didn't want to depart from a winning formula, so sequels of successful films became common. Indiana Jones continued his adventures in *Raiders of the Lost Ark* (1981) with *Indiana Jones and the Temple of Doom* (1984) and *Indiana Jones and the Last Crusade* (1989).[5] Sometimes too many sequels were made and they lost their appeal, as demonstrated by *Police Academy* and its six sequels.

### Celebrity workout videos

In 1982,[6] Jane Fonda started a new trend – the celebrity workout video. She was best known for her Oscar-winning acting, but her fitness video found a new market created by the accessibility of the home video player. This led to a flurry of other celebrities producing their own versions.

All-time box office earnings worldwide for top films made in the 1980s and 1990s

| Ranking (1980-99) | Title | Worldwide earnings in million $ | Year |
| --- | --- | --- | --- |
| 1 | Titanic | $1.8 (billion) | 1997 |
| 2 | Star Wars: Episode I – The Phantom Menace | $925.5 | 1999 |
| 3 | Jurassic Park | $920.1 | 1993 |
| 4 | The Lion King | $822.2 | 1994 |
| 5 | Independence Day | $817.4 | 1996 |
| 6 | E.T.: The Extra-Terrestrial | $792.9 | 1982 |
| 7 | Forrest Gump | $679.7 | 1994 |
| 8 | The Sixth Sense | $672.8 | 1999 |

Even after watching films at home became popular, the megastars of film still attracted people to the cinemas and received ever-increasing wages for it.

Film companies had to work hard to entice those viewers into cinemas who wanted to wait until the films were available on video or DVD. Special effects were one way of doing this because no matter how good the surround sound or picture quality were at home, nothing beats seeing a spectacular visual effect up on the big screen.

Technological developments in computer programming created more and more sophisticated and realistic visual effects in films. Visual effects have been in use since the earliest films, but computer-generated imagery (CGI) took the effects to a new level.

## Science fiction

Science fiction films were perfect for special effects. In the late 1970s, George Lucas created *Star Wars*, using special effects to produce an extraterrestrial world and characters. At the time, the film was considered advanced in terms of special effects, although it was not as sophisticated as today's films. *Star Wars* was incredibly popular and became one of the highest-grossing motion pictures in history, appealing to audiences who weren't necessarily science fiction fans.[7] Lucas produced two other episodes in the *Star Wars* saga, *The Empire Strikes Back* (1980) and *The Return of the Jedi* (1983). By 1997, technology had advanced further, so Lucas added new special effects to these Star Wars films and reissued them. Fans were eager to see Lucas's prequel to the trilogy, *Star Wars: Episode I – The Phantom Menace* in 1999.

A scene from *Star Wars: Episode I–The Phantom Menace*. The special effects succeeded in wowing cinema audiences.

Special effects and computer imagery have also been used to alter the real world. For example, in *Forrest Gump* (1994), historical footage was digitally manipulated to show the film's main character interacting with Richard Nixon, John F. Kennedy, and John Lennon. This film won an Academy Award for Best Visual Effects and was a huge hit despite having a quirky story and not being an all-action blockbuster.

## Merchandising

The film industry was no longer simply about making films. Merchandising had become important in generating revenue. Every big film would have soundtracks, T-shirts and other clothing, games, videos, mugs, and a host of other products available for sale. Films would tie in with fast-food restaurants, soft drinks, and breakfast cereals to promote their products. The whole of the *Star Wars* film series and merchandising is estimated to have brought in about $20 billion.[8] The cost of producing a film, especially a big Hollywood blockbuster, is so high that many films rely on the profits from merchandising to make money.

At a 3-D film in the 1990s, the audience wore special glasses. One lens would be red, the other green.

## 3-D films

Three-dimensional (3-D) films had regained their popularity in the 1980s and 1990s because of the increase in IMAX cinemas. These are special types of cinema that show widescreen films. In the mid-1980s, IMAX began producing non-fiction films in 3-D. To get the 3-D experience, the viewer wears special 3-D glasses.

**29**

# Animation

Animated films were a huge success in the mid-1990s. Disney revived an interest in animation and in Disney itself in 1988[9] with its film *Who Framed Roger Rabbit*, which was a mix of real actors and classic and new cartoon characters. Props were moved around on wires and then the cartoon characters were hand-drawn into the scenes to appear to be using the props. But it was *Toy Story*, in 1995, that really started the craze for animation. *Toy Story* was the first fully computer-animated feature film. It was about Woody, a toy cowboy, who feels threatened and jealous when space ranger Buzz Lightyear appears. *Toy Story* was produced by Pixar Animation Studios and distributed by Disney. It earned its director, John Lasseter, a special Oscar.

# Stop-action

The success of CGI in *Toy Story* changed the way animated films were made. Before CGI, animated films were produced using stop-action, or stop-motion, animation. This was an incredibly time-consuming process whereby the object being animated is moved in tiny amounts between each photographed frame.

# Rush to animate

Following the success of *Toy Story*, film companies such as Disney, Warner Brothers, Twentieth Century Fox, Universal Pictures, and DreamWorks expanded their feature animation division. CGI animation was what the public wanted to see, and successful animation brought in lots of money. In 1998, *A Bug's Life* was the highest-grossing animated release of that year, with about $163 million in the United States and over $362 million worldwide. *Toy Story 2* (1999) broke opening weekend box office records in the United States, the United Kingdom, and Japan, making over $485 million worldwide.[10]

## Aardman Animations

Aardman Animations' film series featuring the characters Wallace and Gromit was an Oscar-winning stop-motion hit. The lovable characters of a quirky inventor and his clever dog and their unexpected adventures in *A Grand Day Out* (1985), *The Wrong Trousers* (1993), and *A Close Shave* (1995) appealed to audiences of all ages. The animation had an old-fashioned feel compared to films such as *Toy Story*, and proved that an independent filmmaker could be popular and successful with an original idea.

**Selected animated film box office earnings for the United States and worldwide**

| Date | Film | US earnings in $ | Worldwide earnings in $ |
|------|------|------------------|-------------------------|
| 1995 | *Toy Story* | $191.8 million | $358.8 million |
| 1998 | *A Bug's Life* | $162.8 million | $358 million |
| 1998 | *Toy Story 2* | $245.8 million | $485.7 million |

Buzz Lightyear and Woody in *Toy Story*. The film started the craze for CGI films in 1995.

# Television

The 1980s and 1990s saw a shift in culture in television. Satellite and digital delivery systems and cable television became more accessible and meant there were many more television channels to choose from. People were no longer watching the same channels as everyone else. There were channels available for a variety of specific audiences. Nevertheless, there were some very definite hit TV programmes.

US television had an enormous influence on television programming around the world. Hit TV shows from the United States dominated television choice. Sitcoms were very popular and hit shows included *Seinfeld* (which became one of the most popular sitcoms of all time), *The Cosby Show*, *Cheers*, *Family Ties*, and *Friends*. The characters from *Friends* greatly influenced fashion, as the "Rachel" haircut became the hairstyle to have in the 1990s.

UK television was also influential with hits such as *Only Fools and Horses*, which introduced sayings such as "you plonker" and "dipstick" into popular culture. The 1980s hit *The Young Ones*, co-written by Ben Elton, presented a new style of sitcoms. It took traditional storylines but used them in a new, surreal, post-punk way. Never before had a flagship comedy programme shown such a degree of violence, squalor, and physical foulness, but it was funny. It showed that comedy was going off in a different direction to where it had been before.[11] Elton teamed up with Richard Curtis (writer of *Four Weddings and a Funeral*) to write *Blackadder*. Set in various times throughout history, *Blackadder* showed that the sitcom could be clever and funny. Blackadder was the ultimate anti-hero who always had a brilliant put-down and "a cunning plan".

*Dynasty* became one of the most popular TV programmes in the mid-eighties.

## Soap operas

*Dallas* and *Dynasty* were two US soap operas that were famous for their flashy show of wealth and huge shoulder pads. Each show was based around a wealthy oil family and featured scheming ex-wives and children.

The showy wealth of *Dallas* and *Dynasty* reflected 1980s aspirations. It was in direct contrast to the British soap operas of the time, such as *EastEnders* and *Brookside*. These soaps reflected the gritty realism of ordinary lives and dealt with often controversial topics such as drug abuse and abortion. *Grange Hill* was the first soap opera aimed specifically at children and it broke new ground in the 1980s tackling real-life issues such as bullying and dyslexia.[12]

Australian soap operas also found success in the United Kingdom. *Home and Away* and *Neighbours* represented a change of target audience, because they appealed to teenage audiences as well as their parents.

### The chat show

The chat show was a popular television format, and it was dominated by one woman – Oprah Winfrey. Her show was nationally **syndicated** in 1986 and became the highest-rated television talk show in the United States.[13]

Oprah Winfrey is one of the most influential women in the United States. She also has her own cable television network and magazine.

# Manga and anime

What do "manga" and "anime" mean? The word *manga* comes from "manga eiga", which means "cartoon movies" in Japanese. Manga refers to Japanese comic strips. People in the Japanese animation industry used the term *animéshon*, meaning "animation", and this has become shortened to "anime".[1] The animation industry in Japan developed along the same timeline as animation in the Western world, during the early 1900s.

Manga and anime have been used for television series, films, video, video games, fiction, commercials, and Internet-based releases. Although it has been popular in Japan for decades, manga and anime grew in worldwide popularity in the 1980s and 1990s, helped by Nintendo's *Pokémon* video game. Manga was made for children and adults. Popular children's characters include Hello Kitty, Pokémon, Astro Boy, and Doraemon.[2]

## The 1980s: The golden age of anime

The 1980s is considered to be the golden age of anime. Two of the major studios, Studio Ghibli and Gainax, were founded in this decade. This was also the decade that saw the rise of the influential directors Mamoru Oshii and Katsuhiro Ótomo.[3] Successful anime included *Nausicaä of the Valley of the Wind*, *Akira*, and *Castle in the Sky*.

## Global success in the 1990s

In the 1990s, the worldwide popularity of anime became more obvious when US fans started to organize their first large-scale conventions, in places such as Dallas and San Jose. The Internet was used by fans to communicate with each other and to spread anime news. Since the Internet was relatively new, people were surprised at how fast and far the news travelled. One website used by fans was Anime Web Turnpike.[4]

### Global influence of anime

Anime has influenced world culture. People started to become more interested in the culture of Japan, and animation studios around the world started to copy the style of Japanese anime. *Avatar: The Last Airbender* is an example of a US animated TV series that was influenced by anime.

## Girl appeal

Most anime appealed to boys, but the creators broadened the audience in the United States and elsewhere by making films and short series aimed at teenage girls. Anime such as *Sailor Moon* (1992–1997), which is about five magical girls who battle demons and incorporates comedy, romance, and tragedy,[5] is responsible for turning a generation of young girls on to anime.

## Manga

The growth of manga comic books in the United States was small until 1987, when *Lone Wolf and Cub* by Kazuo Koike and Goseki Kojima was released. Its success was helped by the covers, which were designed by the influential American comic book artist, writer, and film director Frank Miller.[6]

Today manga is the fastest-growing book category in the United States. In the United Kingdom even Shakespeare and the Bible have been produced in manga-style editions.[7]

An illustration from the manga *Lone Wolf and Cub*.

# The Internet and gaming

Can you imagine not being able to send an email or download the latest music? In 1980, you wouldn't have been able to, since the World Wide Web did not exist.

Internet cafes were set up as places that people could go to surf the Web or check their email while having coffee.

## The Internet's impact

The Internet is a way of allowing various computer networks around the world to connect. It was developed in the 1970s by the US Department of Defence.[1] The World Wide Web is the information retrieval service of the Internet. The Web was developed in 1989 by Tim Berners-Lee and his colleagues at CERN in Geneva, Switzerland. A Web browser was first available to the public in January 1992, and in only two to three years, the Web had millions of active users.[2]

The impact of the Web was immense in changing the way many people lived. In 1995, two influential websites became active: Amazon and eBay.[3] They were two of the first companies to create **e-commerce** websites. Amazon initially sold just books. The success of eBay was partly due to its secure payment procedure. People buying and selling from each other were reassured that their money was safe. At the time there were huge fears about the security of electronic payments.

At first it seemed that doing business using the Internet was the future and nothing could go wrong. People became dot-com millionaires almost overnight, as **venture capitalists** wanted to invest in this new big opportunity. But businesses need solid business plans and to be run properly. Some of these companies were spending money on beautiful, expensive offices and paying high salaries without a real plan for how to make money. Things began to turn sour as investors became more wary and funding stopped. The dot-com bubble burst in 2000,[4] and many people lost a lot of money.

## The Y2K problem

In the late 1990s, people began to worry that when the year 2000 arrived computers would fail. This was because many computer programs had been written to use only the last two digits of the year. Many programs had to be changed at great expense so that the year 2000 wouldn't be registered as 1900. Some people also believed that the world was going to end in the year 2000 and stockpiled food and water. Media companies ran these stories and caused more panic. Of course the world didn't end.

## Gaming

The early 1980s and 1990s saw a rise in electronic gaming as technology advanced and games became more developed. By the end of the 1970s, simple video games could be found in airports, and video arcades started to open, but they didn't become hugely popular until the 1980s, with games like *Space Invaders*. In 1980, *Pac-Man* was introduced and quickly became an international game sensation.[5] Pac-Man is a small, round character, like a pizza with a slice cut out for the mouth. The player has to move Pac-Man through a maze, eating up all the coloured dots while avoiding four ghosts. The game had a big influence on popular culture, and guides on how to play the game made the bestseller lists in the United States. There were also songs, a cartoon series, magazine articles, and other merchandise related to Pac-Man.[6]

## Home video consoles and the PC

Home video consoles, such as the Atari 2600 VCS, that linked into the user's television set were introduced in the late 1970s.[7] Games came on cartridges that were inserted into slots. Young people would go to each other's houses to play games.

*Pac-Man* was a popular arcade game. Players aimed to beat each other's highest score.

The rise in the home computer shifted the direction of video games. Computers allowed a different type of game to develop, which was called interactive fiction or role-playing, and was based on existing print or board games. These games, such as *Dungeons and Dragons* and *The Legend of Zelda*, allowed the user to make choices and control the game narrative. The PC enabled the user to save, creating a deeper game experience, flexible character development, and more complex interactive environments. As the Internet developed, allowing users to play multiplayer versions, Internet communities started becoming established around the popular games.

In the mid- to late 1980s, video consoles were increasing in popularity, with the release of the Nintendo Entertainment System in 1985 and the Sega Genesis in 1989.[8] These new video consoles had graphics that were often better than a PC's. They also had storage cartridges so games could be saved. Sometimes the choice of system would be influenced by the games available to play on them. For example, the iconic game *Sonic the Hedgehog* gave Sega a boost in sales. The handheld Nintendo Game Boy console had the addictive puzzle *Tetris*, which had become an international bestseller, along with the lovable *Mario Brothers* games.

Nintendo's Game Boy quickly sold out when it was released in the United States.

## Did you know?

When Microsoft bundled the card game *Solitaire* with its Windows 3.0, it became one of the most popular games ever.[9]

# The printed word

The exciting development in the written word in the 1990s was how it was delivered. Newspapers, books, and magazines were still available in the traditional paper form, but the growth of the Internet meant people were turning to the World Wide Web for their information.

## Newspapers

In the 1980s and 1990s,[1] traditional newspapers were competing with new formats. Twenty-four hour television news, such as CNN and BBC News, the spread of free newspapers, and the growth of the Internet meant that people started to expect free access to news and also to read today's news today, not tomorrow. TV and the Internet were updated instantly. This threatened newspapers' traditional paid subscriptions. Newspapers started to put content online in the hope that advertising income would be strong. Most initially didn't charge for their online content so that they could compete with these other free sources.

Another trend in newspapers in the early 1980s was that of the national newspaper. Newspapers such as the *Financial Times* and the *Wall Street Journal* took advantage of the new electronic publishing technology to produce national daily newspapers instead of their previous regional ones. The early 1980s also saw the introduction of full-colour newspapers. In 1982, *USA Today* was launched as a full-colour national daily newspaper. In the United Kingdom a similar newspaper was produced called *Today*. It was the first British national newspaper produced using only the new technology. Although it forced the other national newspapers into using colour, *Today* was not a financial success and it closed in 1995.[2]

## Fantasy fiction

The fantasy genre of fiction remained a popular subculture in the 1980s and 1990s, linked to the growth of related games, such as the role-playing game *Dungeons and Dragons* and console games such as *Final Fantasy*. Japanese anime was also part of this fantasy genre (see pages 34–35). Popular fiction of this period included Terry Pratchett's *Discworld* series, Philip Pullman's *His Dark Materials* trilogy, and J. K. Rowling's *Harry Potter* series.

Pictured here with his mother, Stephen Hawking proved that science could be popular too.

## Bestsellers

The year 1988[3] saw scientist Stephen Hawking's *A Brief History of Time: From the Big Bang to Black Holes* top the bestseller lists in the United Kingdom and the United States. The title was on the *Sunday Times* bestseller list in the United Kingdom for an amazing 237 weeks.[4]

# Megamusicals

A musical is a show with song and dance numbers in pop music styles. A megamusical is a musical with lavish stagings, and simultaneous multiple productions around the world. The megamusical is often completely sung or has minimal spoken sections.

## Andrew Lloyd Webber dominates

In the 1980s and 1990s, one name dominated the megamusical scene: Andrew Lloyd Webber. In the 1960s and 1970s, Lloyd Webber collaborated with Tim Rice on the rock opera *Jesus Christ Superstar* (1971) and *Evita* (1978), about Eva Perón, the wife of Argentine dictator Juan Perón.[1] *Jesus Christ Superstar* became the longest-running musical in Britain, and the **Broadway** production of *Evita* won seven **Tony Awards**. The success of these encouraged the production of more musicals. In 1981,[2] Lloyd Webber produced *Cats*, in which verses from a T. S. Eliot children's book were set to music. It became an unexpected international success and was the longest-running show ever on Broadway.[3] Lloyd Webber followed this success with *Starlight Express* (1984),[4] which is famed for the performers wearing roller skates. *Starlight Express* ran in London for over 17 years.[5] Lloyd Webber created *Phantom of the Opera*, which was another great success and, in 1998, won best musical at the Tony Awards. By 2006, it had replaced *Cats* as the longest-running show on Broadway.[6]

By the 1990s,[7] there was a new trend for converting cartoons to musicals. The Walt Disney Company had major successes with its stage re-creations of *Beauty and the Beast* (1994) and *The Lion King* (1998). These shows also provided a new, younger audience with the chance to experience the megamusical.

## Pop-chart success

Lloyd Webber's stage shows also became successful music albums. Songs from his shows were commercially successful in the pop charts, including Boyzone's number one cover version of "No Matter What" and Michael Ball's "Love Changes Everything" from *Aspects of Love*.

*Starlight Express* is a musical about a child's dream in which his toy train set comes to life. The performers all wear roller skates.

# Fashion

In the 1980s, designer clothing was all the rage. Big-name designers included Italians Giorgio Armani, Gianni Versace, Missoni, Franco Moschino, Valentino, and Gianfranco Ferré. In the United States, Ralph Lauren, Calvin Klein, Oscar de la Renta, and Donna Karan all had thriving careers, and in the United Kingdom Vivienne Westwood and Katharine Hamnett were very successful. In 1981, Giorgio Armani launched a "**diffusion**" range called Emporio, which was designer fashion at a slightly lower price.[1] Soon other designers were producing their own diffusion lines. Although they were still expensive, these more affordable fashion lines appealed to those people who had more disposable income during the 1980s. They were influenced by what they saw on TV and in lifestyle magazines, and wanted to look like these designer-label-wearing celebrities.

Gianni Versace and models Carla Bruni (right) and Naomi Campbell (left) pose at a fundraising dinner for the Save the Rainforests organization.

## The megabrand

The 1990s were all about the megabrand. Designers weren't just selling clothes and accessories, they were selling a lifestyle. Ralph Lauren started the trend in the late 1980s by moving into "homewear" such as furniture.[2] Designers such as Armani, Donna Karan, and Ralph Lauren bought restaurants, so a consumer could now eat in designer style as well as wear it.

## The supermodel

The 1980s and 1990s saw the rise of the supermodel. George Michael's music video for *Freedom! '90* grouped together several top models, including Cindy Crawford, Linda Evangelista, Christy Turlington, and Naomi Campbell. These models were then hired by designer Gianni Versace, and this started the trend of the supermodel. These models became celebrities and could be recognized worldwide by just their first name. Their personal appearance often mattered more than what they wore, and their styles were copied by fans.

The 1990s saw the increase in popularity of waiflike models, such as Kate Moss and Amber Valletta, whose slim, almost boyish figures contrasted with those of the curvy supermodels. The size of these models started the debate about models and their effect on girls growing up. There was concern that these waifs were influencing eating disorders in young women.

### Gianni Versace (1946-1997)

Gianni Versace was born in Italy in 1946. He learned his dressmaking skills from his mother. Versace held his first fashion show in 1978, and throughout the 1980s and 1990s built up a fashion empire. His designs were criticized by some people as being flashy and vulgar, but Versace is credited with turning the fashion world into the high-powered, celebrity-obsessed industry it is today. His fashion shows were like rock concerts. They were attended by his celebrity friends, including Madonna and Elton John, and of course his supermodels. On 15 July 1997,[3] Versace was shot and killed on the steps of his Miami Beach home. A huge manhunt was already underway, as the suspect was wanted for killing four other people across the country before Versace. He was eventually found less than three miles from the murder scene. He had committed suicide.[4]

## Power dressing

There was a fashion trend in the 1980s that was all about showing power and wealth. Everything was big, from the hair to the heels to the shoulder pads. Women wore masculine-looking power suits for business to make a statement in the male-dominated workplace. The look was influenced by powerful women such as the British prime minister, Margaret Thatcher, and by Joan Collins and Linda Gray in the television shows *Dynasty* and *Dallas*.

The term *yuppie* stands for "young, upwardly mobile professional" and was used in the early 1980s to describe young people who seemed to make and spend a lot of money and worry about their social status. The stereotypical look for a male yuppie was an expensive pinstripe suit, combined with a skinny tie, red braces, and, later, a chunky mobile phone so they could do business wherever they were. Books such as *The Bonfire of the Vanities* by Tom Wolfe and *Bright Lights, Big City* by Jay McInerney reflected the yuppie lifestyle.

## The influence of TV and film

Television programmes were a big influence on men's fashion in the 1980s. Don Johnson, in *Miami Vice*, popularized the fashion for "designer stubble" worn with a bright- or pastel-coloured T-shirt under a designer jacket, and no socks. Tom Selleck, in *Magnum P.I.*, made the Hawaiian shirt and sports jacket fashionable and started a trend for moustaches.

Films such as *Fame*, *Flashdance*, and *Valley Girl* combined with the aerobics craze set the fashion for leotards, sweatshirts, leg warmers, and ra-ra skirts.

Don Jonson showing the *Miami Vice* look that he made popular in the 1980s.

48

## The preppies and Sloanes

The Sloane look in the United Kingdom and the preppy look in the United States were worn by the upper classes. The preppy look was conservative and favoured the classic single- or double-breasted navy blazer with gold buttons. This was worn with a neat shirt in a solid colour or with candy stripes. More casually, it consisted of a polo shirt (preferably by Ralph Lauren Polo), khaki pants, and loafers.

Sloanes, or Sloane Rangers, were named after fashionable Sloane Square in London. Lady Diana Spencer, the future Princess of Wales, was a leading role model of this look. Lady Di wore the typical Sloane style of frilly, high-necked blouses with puffy sleeves, pearls, floral skirts, and low-heeled shoes. Many people followed the fashions Diana wore, changing their style to match hers.

Lady Diana Spencer was a role model for many women in the 1980s and 1990s.

### Neon colours

To go with the excesses of the 1980s fashions, neon colours became popular. Colours such as shocking pink, turquoise, fluorescent yellow, acid green, and electric blue were on everything from socks to tops. Some of these colours even appeared in mascara. To go with the neon, there was Lycra. Tight Lycra leotards were the fashion during the aerobics craze in the 1980s. Lycra was fashionable as cycling shorts worn under baby-doll dresses or short skirts.

# The influence of music

Youth-orientated fashion was often inspired by musical styles, from hip-hop and heavy metal, to Madonna and other pop stars of the 1980s, to the anti-fashion grunge of the 1990s.

## Hip-hop

The huge influence of hip-hop culture affected fashion as well as music and art. Rappers such as Run-DMC created a new style of dress, consisting of bowler or fedora hats, black tracksuit or leather jackets, unlaced Adidas shell-toe shoes, black jeans, and big gold jewellery. Other fashion basics for the hip-hop look were brand-name tracksuits, sheepskin jackets, baseball caps, and baseball jackets. Women might wear over-sized trousers and checked shirts as worn by R&B singer Aaliyah. Trainers such as Nike's Air Jordan basketball shoes were a big part of the hip-hop look. As the hip-hop style developed, jeans got baggier and saggier to show off the white Calvin Klein underwear. Popular clothing labels were Adidas, Nike, Kangol, and Le Coq Sportif.

Run DMC in New York City in 1985.

### Repurposing the VW badge

The Beastie Boys' Mike D started the craze for wearing a Volkswagen (VW) car badge on a chain as a giant necklace. This sparked outrage as fans copied the look by taking VW badges from cars all over the United States and the United Kingdom.

## Pop

Popstars played a big role in influencing fashion. Madonna's street urchin look from her "Like a Virgin" single and film *Desperately Seeking Susan* had girls and women backcombing their hair, wearing short skirts over leggings, fishnet fingerless gloves, underwear as outerwear, crucifix jewellery, and lots of bracelets. Madonna's changing fashions continued to influence women's fashion throughout the 1980s and 1990s.

Michael Jackson's look for his "Thriller" video was a big influence on men's fashion. He wore a red and black leather jacket and trousers, one glove, and a pair of sunglasses. The new romantic look was inspired by punk fashion and designer Vivienne Westwood, who created the pirate look for Adam and the Ants. Hair was spiky, men wore make-up, especially eyeliner, and the clothing was often outrageous.

## Grunge

The 1990s saw an end to the excesses of the 1980s with the grunge look, inspired by bands such as Nirvana. People wore checked shirts, thermal underwear, band T-shirts, ripped jeans, and either Dr. Martens or Converse high-top trainers. Grunge wasn't about fashion but it did inspire trends. Designers such as Marc Jacobs showed a grunge-inspired collection in the spring of 1993.[5] Designer customers didn't care about grunge, but the style was an international hit with teenagers.

Madonna's street urchin look set the trend for short skirts and leggings, fingerless gloves, and lots of bracelets.

# Changing times

## Change of attitude

The stock market crashes on Wall Street in 1987 and in London in 1992, and the following economic recession, changed the attitude of society. The flashy show of wealth of the early and mid-1980s came to an end. The rise in unemployment and decline in decent wages created what has been called Generation X. It was the first generation unlikely to make more money than their parents. Many in this generation shared feelings of discontent and resentment towards authority. This shared feeling created the right environment for subcultures such as hip-hop and grunge to catch on and spread into the mainstream and popular culture worldwide.

Traders shout orders as the US stock market plummets on Black Monday, 19 October 1987.

## Technological advances

The advance in music technology allowed new sounds to be created and provided new ways to deliver music. In the early 1980s, the new Sony Walkman was hailed as the latest big technological development, but by the end of the decade it seemed old-fashioned compared to the new CDs. By the late 1990s, the CD's future was in question as CD-quality music could be downloaded from the Web. The ease with which music and films could be distributed over the Web caused concerns about copyright and **piracy**. Films and music were being distributed before their official release. The film and music industry called for a change in the law.

New technology such as drum machines, synthesizers, sequencers, and personal computers created new music by enabling musicians to digitally manipulate sounds. New styles such as hip-hop and rap used specially extended versions of tracks with techniques such as scratching and mixing. Out of hip-hop grew house music with the addition of sampling techniques and drum machines. Different subcultures developed around the different music genres. These subcultures often spread worldwide, breaking down barriers such as race, class, or sexual orientation.

The games culture also developed and increased in sophistication during the 1980s and 1990s. These decades saw the change from the simple graphics of games like *Pac-Man* and *Space Invaders* to the more sophisticated graphics of *Mortal Kombat* or *Grand Theft Auto*. The games culture prompted concerns from some members of society about the effect the violence in video games would have on the users. A new rating system was introduced to help warn users of the content included within a game.

# What did the 1980s and 1990s do for us?

The legacy left by hip-hop and subsequent music genres continues to play an important role in music today. Many of the artists popular in the 1980s and 1990s are still involved in the music industry today, although some might now be behind the scenes managing bands or running record labels. Madonna is still an influential artist, and the Beastie Boys released their eighth studio album in 2011. The VW badges have gone, though.

The fashion of the time still influences today's styles as designers look back for inspiration. Many of the big-name designers are still fashionable.

The original Commodore 64 computer. In 2011, a new version was released, although the casing was the only retro part. The rest was a modern PC.

Personal computers have made huge advances technologically, but a rising fashion for nostalgia has led to the 2011 comeback of the Commodore 64 computer.[1] In 1984, Apple Computer released the first Macintosh, which was the first home computer to feature an easy-to-use operating system and one of the first to offer a mouse. The advertisement that introduced the Macintosh first aired during the Super Bowl, a huge sports event in the United States, and is considered to be one of the best television adverts ever made.

Gaming technology is much more advanced today, but there is still nostalgia for early games. Today there are websites devoted to classic arcade games such as *Pac-Man*, *Donkey Kong*, and *Sonic the Hedgehog*.

The popularity of CGI animation continues with the successful 2010 release of *Toy Story 3*. The trend for all things eighties was also seen in 2010, when a remake of the 1984 film *Karate Kid* and a film based on the popular TV series *The A-Team* were released.

In the 1990s, the Internet and the Web had a huge impact on popular culture and the way people could live their lives. The Web allowed people to communicate with others across the world by way of emails, blogs, and chat rooms. Fans of Japanese anime demonstrated the power of the Web by organizing large-scale conventions and spreading anime news. It is hard to imagine a world without the Web. Where would we be without it? Websites such as Amazon and eBay, which have been around since the early Internet days, have expanded into different areas as they have become more successful. The increase in retail purchasing online has affected delivery companies because more people are shopping this way. It is now possible to buy almost anything online. Many lessons have been learned the hard way about how to operate a successful online company.

Technological advances since the 1990s have further improved Internet communication. Programs such as Skype allow people to communicate for free and even to see each other over their computer screens. Today, access to the Web can be made through mobile phones using free Wi-Fi, something the yuppies of the 1980s would have loved!

# Timeline

**May 1979**
Margaret Thatcher becomes Britain's first female prime minister.

**1979**
The Sony Walkman is released.

**1980**
The compact disc (CD) is introduced.

**December 1980**
John Lennon is shot dead in New York.

**1980–1988**
Iran-Iraq War sees some of the heaviest fighting on land since World War II.

**1981**
"The Adventures of Grandmaster Flash on the Wheels of Steel" showcases the new sound of scratching.

**February 1981**
Prince Charles and Lady Diana Spencer announce their engagement. They are married on 29 July 1981.

**August 1981**
MTV begins broadcasting music videos in the United States.

**1984**
Apple Computer introduces the Macintosh home computer.

**July 1985**
Live Aid concert held simultaneously in London and Philadelphia.

**January 1986**
US space shuttle *Challenger* disaster.

**1987**
Guns N' Roses album *Appetite for Destruction* released.

**1987**
Black Monday, 19 October, Wall Street crash ends an era of economic prosperity.

**December 1988**
The bombing of Pan Am Flight 103 over Lockerbie, Scotland, kills 270 people.

**June 1989**
Students hold a pro-democracy demonstration in Tiananmen Square, Bejing.

**November 1989**
Berlin Wall comes down.

**1989**
George H. W. Bush becomes US president.

**1989**
The World Wide Web is developed by Tim Berners-Lee and his colleagues at CERN.

**August 1990–February 1991**
First Gulf War.

**1990**
Mikhail Gorbachev becomes president of the Soviet Union.

**1991**
Collapse of the Soviet Union.

**1991–1995**
Yugoslavian civil war.

**1991**
Nirvana's *Nevermind* album is released and receives global attention.

**September 1992**
Black Wednesday, 16 September, London's stock exchange crashes.

**1993**
Bill Clinton becomes US president.

**April 1994**
First multi-race election held in South Africa; Nelson Mandela voted in as president.

**April 1994**
Kurt Cobain commits suicide.

**1995**
*Toy Story* is the first feature film to be made entirely with CGI.

**May 1997**
Tony Blair becomes the British prime minister.

**August 1997**
Diana, Princess of Wales, is killed in a car crash in Paris.

**1999**
Balkan War.

# Best of the era

The best way to find out about the pop culture of the 1980s and 1990s is to experience it for yourself. Here are some suggestions for the best or most typical examples that will give you a sense of the time.

## Music
*Definitely Maybe* by Oasis
*Everything Changes* by Take That
*Low Life* by New Order
*Nevermind* by Nirvana
*Spice* by Spice Girls
*Thriller* by Michael Jackson

## Television
*The A-Team*
*Blackadder*
*Dynasty*
*Knight Rider*
*Seinfeld*
*The Young Ones*

## Films
*Forrest Gump*
*The Empire Strikes Back*
*Titanic*
*Toy Story*

## Video games
*Donkey Kong*
*Pac-Man*
*Super Mario Brothers*

# Notes on sources

## What is popular culture?

1. http://www.ft.com/indepth/blackmonday, Accessed 13 June 2011.

2. http://news.bbc.co.uk/1/hi/business/2259648.stm, Accessed 13 June 2011.

3. "Thatcher, Margaret", *Encyclopædia Britannica, Encyclopædia Britannica Online Library Edition, Encyclopædia Britannica*, 2011, http://library.eb.co.uk/eb/article-214939, Accessed 14 June 2011.

4. "Clinton, Bill", *Encyclopædia Britannica, Encyclopædia Britannica Online Library Edition, Encyclopædia Britannica*, Inc., 2011, http://library.eb.co.uk/eb/article-9003019, Accessed 26 July 2011.

5. "Blair, Tony", *Encyclopædia Britannica, Encyclopædia Britannica Online Library Editio, Encyclopædia Britannica*, Inc., 2011, http://library.eb.co.uk/eb/article-9003134, Accessed 26 July 2011.

6. "Berlin Wall", *Encyclopædia Britannica, Encyclopædia Britannica Online Library Edition, Encyclopædia Britannica*, 2011, http://library.eb.co.uk/eb/article-9078806, Accessed 14 June 2011.

7. Chris Cook and John Stevenson, *The Routledge Companion to World History Since 1914*, UK: Routledge, 2005, 328.

8. http://www.world-nuclear.org/info/chernobyl/inf07.html, Accessed 20 January 2012.

## Music

1. "Pop", Grove Music Online, Oxford University Press, 2011, http://www.oxfordmusiconline.com/subscriber/article/grove/music/46845?q=pop&source=omo_t237&source=omo_gmo&source=omo_t114&search=quick&pos=1&_start=1#firsthit, Accessed 6 June 2011.

2. "Pop", Grove Music Online.

3. "Pop", Grove Music Online.

4. "Pop", Grove Music Online.

5. Cook and Stevenson, *The Routledge Companion to World History Since 1914*, 398.

6. Cook and Stevenson, *The Routledge Companion to World History Since 1914*, 398.

7. "Sony Corporation", *Encyclopædia Britannica, Encyclopedia Britannica Online Library Edition, Encyclopædia Britannica*, 2011, http://library.eb.co.uk/eb/article-280842, Accessed 7 June 2011.

8. http://www.oxfordmusiconline.com/subscriber/article/grove/music/46845?qa=computer&search=search_in_article#hit_in_article1, 7/26/11.

9. "Live Aid", *Encyclopædia Britannica, Encyclopedia Britannica Online Library Edition, Encyclopædia Britannica*, 2011, http://library.eb.co.uk/eb/article-9488745, accessed 6 June 2011.

10. "House", *Encyclopædia Britannica, Encyclopædia Britannica Online Library Edition, Encyclopædia Britannica*, 2011, http://library.eb.co.uk/eb/article-9097024, Accessed 11 July 2011.

11. "Dance music", Grove Music Online, http://www.oxfordmusiconline.com/subscriber/article/grove/music/47215, Accessed 7 June 2011.

12. "The Warehouse", *Encyclopædia Britannica, Encyclopædia Britannica Online Library Edition, Encyclopædia Britannica*, 2011, http://library.eb.co.uk/eb/article-9118534, Accessed 26 July 2011.

13. "Dance music", Grove Music Online.

14. "Dance music", Grove Music Online.

15. "How Tony Wilson Changed Music", BBC News, 2007, http://news.bbc.co.uk/1/hi/entertainment/6941846.stm.

16. http://news.bbc.co.uk/1/hi/entertainment/6941846.stm.

17. "Pop", Grove Music Online.

18. "Grunge", Grove Music Online, http://www.oxfordmusiconline.com/subscriber/article/grove/music/49139?q=grunge&search=quick&pos=1&_start=1#firsthit, Accessed 7 June 2011.

19. "Punk", *Encyclopædia Britannica, Encyclopedia Britannica Online Library Edition, Encyclopædia Britannica*, 2011, http://library.eb.co.uk/eb/article-9099010, Accessed 7 June 2011.

20. "Pop", Grove Music Online.

21. "Nirvana", *Encyclopædia Britannica, Encyclopedia Britannica Online Library Edition, Encyclopædia Britannica*, 2011, http://library.eb.co.uk/eb/article-9105679, Accessed 7 June 2011.

22. "Looking Back at the Birth of Britpop", BBC News, 15 August 2005, http://news.bbc.co.uk/1/hi/entertainment/music/4144458.stm, Accessed 7 June 2011.

23. Looking back at the birth of Britpop, BBC News.

24. "Britpop", Grove Music Online, http://www.oxfordmusiconline.com/subscriber/article/grove/music/46596, Accessed 7 June 2011.

25. "Britpop", Grove Music Online.

26. http://www.bbc.co.uk/music/sevenages/events/indie/blur-vs-oasis, Accessed 7 June 2011.

27. "Graham Coxon Nearly Driven to Suicide By Blur vs Oasis Chart Battle", Music World, 8 May 2009. http://www.themusic-world.com/news/14454.

28. "Oasis", Grove Music Online. http://www.oxfordmusiconline.com/subscriber/article/grove/music/46603?q=oasis&search=quick&pos=1&_start=1#firsthit, Accessed 7 June 2011.

## Hip-hop, New York style

1. "Hip-hop", *Encyclopædia Britannica, Encyclopedia Britannica Online Library Edition, Encyclopædia Britannica*, 2011, http://library.eb.co.uk/eb/article-288175, Accessed 6 June 2011.

2. "Hip-hop," *Encyclopædia Britannica*.

3. http://www.reuters.com/article/2011/05/28/us-scottheron-idUSTRE74R0CX20110528, Accessed 26 July 2011.

## Art

1. "The Curse of 'Man and Baby': Athena, and the Birth of a Legend", Independent, 16 January 2007, http://www.independent.co.uk/news/uk/this-britain/the-curse-of-man-and-baby-athena-and-the-birth-of-a-legend-432331.html.

2. http://www.jeffkoons.com/site/index.html

3. http://www.sfmoma.org/explore/collection/artwork/187 8/6/11

4. "Richard Prince", Grove Art Online, Oxford University Press, 2011, http://www.oxfordartonline.com/subscriber/article/grove/art/T096941?q=richard+prince&search=quick&pos=2&_start=1#firsthit, Accessed 8 June 2011.

5. "Young British Artists", Grove Art Online, 2011, http://www.oxfordartonline.com/subscriber/article/grove/art/T096668?q=britart&search=quick&pos=2&_start=1#firsthit, Accessed 8 June 2011.

6. http://news.bbc.co.uk/1/hi/entertainment/189585.stm, Accessed 27 July 2011.

7. "Hirst, Damien", *Britannica Book of the Year, 1997, Encyclopedia Britannica Online Library Edition, Encyclopædia Britannica*, 2011,

http://library.eb.co.uk/eb/article-9112977, Accessed 8 June 2011; http://news.bbc.co.uk/1/hi/in_depth/uk/2000/newsmakers/2268841.stm, Accessed July 27, 2011.

8. http://www.oxfordartonline.com/subscriber/article/grove/art/T094002?q=hirst&search=quick&pos=2&_start=1#firsthit.

9. Henry Chalfant and James Prigoff, *Spraycan Art*, London: Thames & Hudson, reprinted 2006, 7.

10. Chalfant and Prigoff, *Spraycan Art*, 7.

11. Chalfant and Prigoff, *Spraycan Art*, 10, 60.

12. "Basquiat, Jean-Michel", *Encyclopædia Britannica, Encyclopedia Britannica Online Library Edition, Encyclopædia Britannica*, 2011, http://library.eb.co.uk/eb/article-9435776, Accessed 6 June 2011.

13. "Haring, Keith," *Encyclopædia Britannica, Encyclopedia Britannica Online Library Edition, Encyclopædia Britannica*, 2011, http://library.eb.co.uk/eb/article-9435727, Accessed 26 July 2011.

## Film and TV

1. Cook and Stevenson, *The Routledge Companion to World History Since 1914*, 398.

2. http://www.dolby.co.uk/about/who-we-are/our-history/history-4.html.

3. "Computers and Information Systems", *Encyclopædia Britannica, Encyclopedia Britannica Online Library Edition, Encyclopædia Britannica*, 2011, http://library.eb.co.uk/eb/article-91785, Accessed 9 June 2011.

4. http://news.bbc.co.uk/1/hi/entertainment/2787117.stm, Accessed 27 July 2011.

5. "Indiana Jones", *Encyclopædia Britannica, Encyclopedia Britannica Online Library Edition, Encyclopædia Britannica*, 2011, http://library.eb.co.uk/eb/article-9443836, Accessed 8 June 2011.

6. Do Any Celebrity Workout Videos Actually Work?, USA Today, 26 January 2005,

http://www.usatoday.com/life/columnist/popcandy/2005-01-25-pop-candy_x.htm.

7. "Lucas, George", *Encyclopædia Britannica, Encyclopedia Britannica Online Library Edition, Encyclopædia Britannica*, 2011, http://library.eb.co.uk/eb/article-9049231, Accessed 9 June 2011.

8. "Star Wars", *Encyclopædia Britannica, Encyclopedia Britannica Online Library Edition, Encyclopædia Britannica*, 2011, http://library.eb.co.uk/eb/article-9443000, Accessed 9 June 2011.

9. Richard Rickitt and Ray Harryhausen, *Special Effects: The History and Technique*, London: Aurum Press Ltd., 2006, 367.

10. http://www.pixar.com/companyinfo/history/86.html, Accessed 5 April 2011

11. http://www.bbc.co.uk/comedy/theyoungones/, Accessed 27 July 2011.

12. http://www.grangehillfans.co.uk/history/potted.php, Accessed 27 July 2011.

13. "Winfrey, Oprah", *Encyclopædia Britannica, Encyclopedia Britannica Online Library Edition, Encyclopædia Britannica*, 2011, http://library.eb.co.uk/eb/article-9002504, Accessed 8 June 2011.

## Manga and anime

1. Simon Richmond, *The Rough Guide to Anime*, London: Rough Guides, 2009.

2. Richmond, *The Rough Guide to Anime*, 17.

3 Richmond, *The Rough Guide to Anime*, 20.

4 Richmond, *The Rough Guide to Anime*, 24.

5 Richmond, *The Rough Guide to Anime*, 210.

6 Richmond, *The Rough Guide to Anime*, 184.

7 Richmond, *The Rough Guide to Anime*, 184.

## The Internet and gaming

1. "Internet", *Encyclopædia Britannica, Encyclopædia Britannica Online Library Edition, Encyclopædia Britannica, 2011*, http://library.eb.co.uk/eb/article-218350, Accessed 11 June 2011.

2. "World Wide Web", *Encyclopædia Britannica, Encyclopædia Britannica Online Library Edition, Encyclopædia Britannica, 2011*, http://library.eb.co.uk/eb/article-9002506, Accessed 11 June 2011.

3. Amazon.com, http://phx.corporate-ir.net/phoenix.zhtml?c=176060&p=irol-corporateTimeline, Accessed 12 June 2011; "eBay," *Encyclopædia Britannica, Encyclopædia Britannica Online Library Edition, Encyclopædia Britannica, 2011*.

http://library.eb.co.uk/eb/article-9438594, Accessed 12 June 2011.

4. Dot.com to Dot.bomb, *BBC News*, 15 December 2000,

http://news.bbc.co.uk/1/hi/in_depth/business/2000/review/1069169.stm, Accessed 12 June 2011.

5. "Pac-Man", *Encyclopædia Britannica, Encyclopædia Britannica Online Library Edition, Encyclopædia Britannica, 2011*, http://library.eb.co.uk/eb/article-9389964, Accessed 12 June 2011.

6. "Pac-Man", *Encyclopædia Britannica.*

7. "Electronic game", *Encyclopædia Britannica, Encyclopædia Britannica Online Library Edition, Encyclopædia Britannica, 2011*, http://library.eb.co.uk/eb/article-233728, Accessed 12 June 2011.

8. "Electronic game", *Encyclopædia Britannica, Encyclopædia Britannica Online Library Edition, Encyclopædia Britannica, 2011*, http://library.eb.co.uk/eb/article-233731, Accessed 12 June 2011.

9. http://www.icheg.org/research, Accessed 12 June 2011.

## The printed word

1. "Publishing, history of", *Encyclopædia Britannica, Encyclopædia Britannica Online Library Edition, Encyclopædia Britannica, 2011*, http://library.eb.co.uk/eb/article-236526, Accessed 13 June 2011.

2. "Publishing, history of", *Encyclopædia Britannica*, http://library.eb.co.uk/eb/article-236525, Accessed 13 June 2011.

3. "Hawking, Stephen W.", *Encyclopædia Britannica, Encyclopædia Britannica Online Library Edition, Encyclopædia Britannica, 2011*, http://library.eb.co.uk/eb/article-9039612, Accessed 13 June 2011.

4. Tim Radford, "How God Propelled Stephen Hawking into the Bestsellers Lists", *Guardian*, July 31, 2009, http://www.guardian.co.uk/science/2009/jul/30/stephen-hawking-brief-history-time.

## Megamusicals

1. "Lloyd Webber, Andrew, Baron Lloyd-Webber of Sydmonton", *Encyclopædia Britannica, Encyclopædia Britannica Online Library Edition, Encyclopædia Britannica, 2011*, http://library.eb.co.uk/eb/article-9048647, Accessed 11 June 2011.

2. "Lloyd Webber, Andrew", *Encyclopædia Britannica.*

3. "Lloyd Webber, Andrew", *Encyclopædia Britannica.*

4. "Lloyd Webber, Andrew", *Encyclopædia Britannica.*

5. "Lloyd Webber, Andrew", *Encyclopædia Britannica.*

6. "Lloyd Webber, Andrew", *Encyclopædia Britannica.*

7. "Musicals", *Grove Music Online*, http://www.oxfordmusiconline.com/subscriber/article/grove/music/19420?q=les+miserables&search=quick&pos=18&_start=1#firsthit, Accessed 11 June 2011.

## Fashion

1. Bronwyn Cosgrave, *Costume and Fashion: A Complete History*, London: Hamlyn, 2003, 235.

2. Bronwyn Cosgrave, *Costume and Fashion*, 237.

3. "Versace, Gianni", *Encyclopædia Britannica, Encyclopædia Britannica Online Library Edition, Encyclopædia Britannica, 2011*, http://library.eb.co.uk/eb/article-9344989, Accessed 27 July 2011.

4. http://news.bbc.co.uk/onthisday/hi/dates/stories/july/15/newsid_2503000/2503757.stm, Accessed 27 July 2011.

5. "Grunge, a Fleeting Fashion Rage", *Britannica Book of the Year*, 1994, *Encyclopædia Britannica Online Library Edition, Encyclopædia Britannica, 2011*, http://library.eb.co.uk/eb/article-9114063, Accessed 13 June 2011.

## What did the 1980s and 1990s do for us?

1. "Classic Commodore 64 Lives Again", *BBC News*, 7 April 2011,

http://www.bbc.co.uk/news/technology-12997245, Accessed 14 June 2011.

# Find out more

## Books

*1980s* (I Can Remember), Sally Hewitt (Franklin Watts, 2010)

*The Berlin Wall* (A Place In History), Richard Tames (Franklin Watts, 2011)

*Entertainment and Gaming* (Mastering Media), Stergios Botzakis (Raintree, 2011)

*Graffiti* (Culture in Action), Jane Bingham (Raintree, 2010)

*Hip-Hop* (Culture in Action), Jim Mack (Raintree, 2010)

*Popular Culture* (Britain Since 1948), Stewart Ross (Wayland, 2010)

*Replay: The History of Video Games*, Tristan Donovan (Yellow Ant, 2010)

## Websites

**www.dondiwhitefoundation.org/index.htm**
Read about the life and work of leading graffiti artist, Dondi White.

**www.dreamworksanimation.com**
Find out how films are animated.

**www.google.com/pacman**
Try this free Google version of the early video game sensation, *Pac-Man*.

**henrychalfant.com/trains**
Gain a deeper insight into the work of graffiti artists and see some of their work as recorded by Henry Chalfant.

**www.icheg.org/game-history**
Read about video game history.

**www.sfmoma.org/explore/multimedia/interactive_features/44**
Find out more about the art of the late twentieth century at the
San Francisco Museum of Modern Art online.

**www.starwars.com**
Find out all about the films and even learn how to draw some of
the characters from *Star Wars*.

## Topics for further research

- Investigate the relationship between the United Kingdom,
  the United States, and the Soviet Union during the Cold War
  to find out how the collapse of communism changed the
  world.

- Research the First Gulf War and find out how history seemed
  to be repeating itself in the Second Gulf War.

- Explore the world of animation and special effects.

# Glossary

**boom box**  portable stereo

**borough**  district of New York City

**break beat**  part of a dance record where only the drums play

**Broadway**  street in New York City where there are lots of theatres

**Cold War**  tense stand-off between democratic countries such as the United States and the United Kingdom and the communist nations led by the Soviet Union. The Cold War began in 1946 (shortly after the end of World War II) and ended with the fall of the Soviet Union in 1991.

**diffusion**  in fashion, designer clothing line priced slightly lower to appeal to a wider variety of consumers

**DIY ethic**  way of thinking that means a person wants to do everything themselves

**e-commerce**  selling goods online

**genre**  type

**hip-hop**  started as an underground culture that included DJing, rapping, break dancing, and graffiti

**immigrant**  person coming to live in another country

**improvise**  create something on the spot

**piracy**  illegal copying or use of copyrighted material, such as films or music

**roadie**  someone who helps bands on tour set up for their gigs

**sampling**  using samples of other songs in music

**scratching**  sliding a record forwards and backwards under a needle

**ska**  style of urban pop from Jamaica

**subculture**  shared lifestyle of a substantial minority within a larger culture

**syndicated** associated with a group of individuals or organizations. A television programme becomes syndicated when it is sold to many local networks.

**tagging** writing a name

**Tony Award** annual award for achievements in American theatre

**Turner Prize** important prize in the art world

**turntable** part of a sound system where a record is played

**venture capitalist** person who puts up money for innovative projects in the hope of making more money

**YBAs** stands for "Young British Artists"

**yuppie** stands for "young, upwardly mobile professional"

# Index